MY VOICE BECAUSE OF YOU

MY VOICE BECAUSE OF YOU

PEDRO SALINAS

Translation and Introduction by
WILLIS BARNSTONE

Preface by
JORGE GUILLÉN

STATE UNIVERSITY OF NEW YORK PRESS
Albany 1976

UNESCO COLLECTION OF REPRESENTATIVE WORKS
EUROPEAN SERIES

This book has been accepted in the series of translations of
European Literature sponsored by the United Nations
Educational, Scientific and Cultural Organization (UNESCO).

My Voice Because of You

Originally published in 1933 as **La voz a ti debida** by
Los Cuatro Vientos

Published by State University of New York Press
99 Washington Avenue, Albany, New York 12210

Translation © 1976 State University of New York
All rights reserved

Printed in the United States of America

Library of Congress Cataloging in Publication Data

Salinas, Pedro, 1892-1951.
My voice because of you.

(UNESCO collection of representative works: European series)
Translation of La voz a ti debida.
Poems.
I. Barnstone, Willis, 1927-   tr. II. Title.
III. Series.
PQ6635.A32V613   1974   861'.6'2   74-14664
ISBN 0-87395-285-5
ISBN 0-87395-287-1 (micro.)

Contents

Preface

I

The work of Pedro Salinas reaches its summit in the theme of love. Has there been any love poetry written in the twentieth century more important than *My Voice Because of You?*

Lovers live alone, seeking and finding each other, happy and anguished, in their own insular spheres. It is always like that. Are there any lovers who are not, or do not wish to be, the sole inhabitants of an island closed off to the rest of the world? For they are the world. This is not poetry of extravagant love but of the most normal love in a completely normal story, and the story is confined to situations of fervid feeling that never slide into sentimentality. They unfold in an analytical description that is deeply thought and felt: thought, passion, tenderness and sensuality fuse together perfectly in a poetry of intensely uniform words. The voice because of love is passionate as a result of anxious searching. Where does the constant hunger come from? There is no social conflict. At such times society does not exist. Is there an internal conflict? No. The lover begins from love—a love he had once—toward the *amada* (the woman loved), toward the best possible *amada*.

II

I, you: that is all. Salinas completes, intensifies, elevates the situation without weakening its normality:

> It's that I want to take out
> of you the best you.

And so the woman—nameless now—becomes a you that implies some kind of mysterious Beyond. Then he discards the figure of a love who might become a deity, under whose power he might suffer. The *I* and *you* share the atmosphere of an Eros that is not a god but a newly created circumference of love. The "first trembling" is immediately confirmed. It is a Genesis with its primal freshness:

> What a sinless day!
> Foam, hour after hour,
> untiringly . . . .

It is not a garden. It is a beach. And suddenly there is a felicitous liveliness:

> Yes, everything in excess:
> light, life, the sea!
> All plural, plural,
> lights, lives, and seas.

The lovers give themselves

> blind . . .
> to a vast risky depth [that
>   sings] :
> "This is nothing yet.
> Look deeply at your selves.
>   There's more."

The heart hurls itself into this quest with pleasant and painful hunger, far from any simple cerebral entertainment. Of course these anxieties are both felt and thought. In lines already famous, he writes:

> To live I don't want
> islands, palaces, towers.
> What steeper joy
> than living in pronouns!

Pronouns, the skeletal grammatical word. The ingenious poet uses them with irony. Are the pronouns *I, you,* metaphysical entities? These monosyllabic condensations reveal the lovers' profound essence that will always exist. The lover says with the greatest simplicity:

> I want you, yes, I'm the one.

It is love that discloses—and creates—the two lovers. A new *I* wants to become a new *you. I, you:* the relationship of all lovers, which in this instance acquires extraordinary height and depth.

III

> I want you pure, free,
> irreducible: you.

A chimera of Platonic perfection is not sought here. Rather, what is longed for is the most profound, secret *you* that love can reveal and exalt, as if that love were dreamt in the "pure, unmoving center in you." This moment of ecstatic calm implies a now unreal hyperbole of the quest that no single plenitude or intoxication can satisfy. It is the extreme Beyond of great demanding love. The lover is not wildly desirous because of the Idea of an inaccessible Laura. His anguished longing corresponds precisely to the reality enjoyed and suffered. It corresponds to plain realism. Will the restlessness ever end? We read: "I don't know where to find you," where to find the *you* that the lover pursues; and the speaker continues, with a simple hyperbole: "shouting or with only the wings of silence" as he pursues the other being who is sinking into herself:

> To ask you to love me
> is to ask for you . . .
> to go
> even further
> than the ultimate
> mines of your being,

the true, the truest ones. So there is a kind of gravitational pull toward the earth:

> . . . Look for weights,
> the deepest in you, so they can
>   drag you down
> to the great center where I
>   wait for you.
> Total love, wanting each other
>   like masses.

IV

Idealism? There is no conflict between passion and behavior. Rather, a vibrating tension: the aim of surpassing the physical zone in the physical zone itself. There is no idyll or drama here, but a quivering loving fullness: "the irreducible you, a naked certain Venus." Nothing is avoided.

> I don't want you to go,
> pain, last form
> of loving . . . .

The story already has a past:

> we have lived together
> in fragile delicate worlds.

Separation reduces the lovers to their own shadows. Remember the last extraordinary poem of *My Voice Because of You:*

> Do you hear how they beg for
>   realities,
> those dishevelled terrible
> shadows that we both make up
> in this great bed of distances?

The question is energetically directed to the absent, remote woman (*amada*). In a poem of absence. A concrete demand for "realities" rises from the poem.

All phantasmagoria is now excluded. And the end:

> . . . return again
> to a mortal and rose body
> where love invents its infinity.

"Corporality" is an abstract noun, yet not a dry concept, thanks to the rose color that evokes the image of a gloriously naked body lying down, "O, mortal" body with its melancholy perspective. The very serene and tender inclination to the concrete slips in where love invents its infinity. A Platonic Idea never hangs over the lovers like a Holy Ghost. Following his profane path a poet today cannot emulate Saint John of the Cross. The journey is taken, knowing that "Infinity" station is never reached. Love traces out the route, that's all: road, "method," no round trip—toward a horizontal nakedness, under a sky that contains all and has no end.

V

The poetry of Salinas perfectly embodies the sinuosity of his thought-feeling. The rational thread is never lost, and he finds the necessary means to make diction explicit. Images and explanations do not impede the course and, if needed, they produce their own explanations. In short, who but an obtuse critic could reduce to reason a whole poetic world? In this case we have the text of the first poet recreated by the second, Willis Barnstone, a poet extremely sensitive to ancient and modern poetry, the interpretor of The Song of Songs, Sappho, Saint John of the Cross, and other diverse figures, among whom the most recent are Antonio Machado and Mao Tse-tung, and who has the insight of a truly modern poet and critic.

Jorge Guillén

Introduction

In 1898 Spain was ingloriously defeated in a war with the United States. The last illusions of empire vanished, and somehow this coincided with an intellectual, artistic and political awakening that has been called the Generation of 1898. No one wrote more lucidly of the common notions of this generation than Pedro Salinas in his volume of essays *Literatura espanola siglo XX*. He saw the "patrician dignity" of the Castilian peasant and spoke of the regeneration of ideas and art in the works of Antonio Machado, Azorín, Miguel de Unamuno.

But Salinas began to write some two decades later and is associated with another group of Spanish poets called the Generation of 1927. It included Rafael Alberti, Federico García Lorca, Jorge Guillén, Luis Cernuda, Vicente Aleixandre—a brilliant, diverse group of poets who were broadly eclectic in their interests. Like other vanguard movements in Europe, they tended to reject the immediate past, but unlike their counterparts elsewhere, they did return consciously to several earlier periods of their native literature, and through this they showed their modernity. So we have the popularism of Alberti and García Lorca, based on folk music and anonymous fifteenth-century songs and ballads, or we have Jorge Guillén, who found the title and partial model for his first major work, *Cántico*, in Saint John of the Cross's *Cántico espiritual*. Pedro Salinas took the title of this collection, *La voz a ti debida*, My Voice Because of You, from a line of the Renaissance poet Garcilaso de la Vega, and went to a medieval lyric, *Razón de amor*, Love's Discourse, for his next volume. The writer, whose three hundredth anniversary in 1927 gave the generation its name, was the Spanish baroque poet Luis de Góngora.

The attempt to rehabilitate Góngora began with some fanfare. There was a pilgrimage to Seville, financed by Ignacio Sánchez Mejías, the bullfighter who was later the subject of Lorca's famous elegy "Llanto por Ignacio Sánchez Mejías." Lorca himself gave a lecture on Góngora at the Ateneo in Seville. This was followed by a pioneering explication of Góngora's difficult poetry by the poet-scholar Dámaso Alonso. The cult of Góngora coincided with a moving away from the immediate past. In his elemental and symbolic snows, diamonds, feathers, metals, Góngora provided fresh imagery and a natural link with a modified surrealism for poets who were weary of the esthetic mistiness and sentimentality of Spanish modernism. Góngora used hyperbole and hyperbatons, and extended the linguistic and musical limits of the Spanish language. All this hard-edged sensorial poetry—with very few ideas that the followers cared about—was both hermetic and crisply extravagant, and became a perfect weapon of modernity.

Poets took from Góngora what they wanted, and no one of that remarkable generation can be accused of mannerism. Alberti composed a "Fragment of the Third Solitude" in imitation of Góngora's *Las soledades*, and Guillén wrote a tribute to don Luis in his *décima* "The Nightingale." Salinas developed independently, without self-conscious imitation or tributes. Yet at times in his clear but convoluted images and ideas, he has a perhaps more natural affinity with Spanish baroque complexity.* So we read:

> . . . lightning rays
> of stork feathers
> so snowy they fall
> flake by flake covering
> the earth in an enormous
> white yes.

or in describing the routes of lovers who wander through the world:

> A jumbled universe:
> minerals in flower
> sailing through the sky,
> sirens and coral
> in perpetual snow,
> and on the sea floor
> constellations
> tired now, fugitives
> in the great orphan night
> where divers die.

---

*The Spanish baroque has been reductively separated into schools of *conceptismo* (play of ideas) often associated with Francisco de Quevedo (1580-1645) and *culteranismo* (play of sounds, images, syntax, lexicon) associated with Luis de Góngora (1561-1627). The separations are of course artificial and only suggest emphasis.

In these early years of his formation, he also likes to turn his mind to such things as typewriter keys, which he calls Underwood girls, thirty nymphs, whose pure deed is wordless, senseless, simply such letters as s, z, j, i. Objects and people are frequently interchangeable, for the poet's central myth is the love of reality: a love as often ironic and humorous as passionate and painful. With love as the energy behind his vision, he moves easily from an outrageously funny and intricate poem about a lightbulb (which he describes as an electric princess in a crystal palace, guarded by a hundred thousand lances of light) to the real girl he hunts for in alphabets and dictionaries and who ultimately talks to him when he is least prepared. The interest in the concrete world of technology, of car radiators and movie screens, is characteristic of the radical literary *isms* of those early decades, and Salinas was particularly fond of the telephone. Indeed, his speech in early (and later) work is often easy and exact, meaningful on several levels, with the intimate, colloquial tone of a phone call, or should we say a telephone meditation.

Salinas's many talents and assimilated influences from the totality of the Spanish Lyric past came together in the sequence of love poems, *La voz a ti debida*, which was published in Madrid in 1933. In linking separate, untitled poems together as a journal of an experience, he solved some basic structural problems inherent in most collections of poetry: how to lead the reader, as in a novel or a play, from beginning to end; how to reinforce through context each separate poem; how to relate a complicated experience of novel or novella proportions in one book of verse.

Rainer Maria Rilke and Federico García Lorca also used a sequence of poems, *Die Sonette an Orpheus* and the *Romancero gitano*, to convey recurrent motifs. The alternative, a single long poem, is very difficult to sustain. Perhaps E.A. Robinson wrote the last book-length poems that hold up. But in a sequence, the poems work both individually and cumulatively. By the end of *My Voice Because of You*, the persona in the series speaks with extraordinary power.

Pedro Salinas speaks with many voices, for the love he details is complex and has many phases. Above all he celebrates the amazement of awakening to the *amada* (the woman). And he returns to the enigmas of the experience, even when love is a shadow. The woman he kisses and hugs and lives with in the air, horizontally, under sea foam, remains metaphysically intact throughout. She does not disappear, even when she is memory and pain; and so the poems are never simply self-awareness but represent, as Jorge Guillén has written, both *I* and *you*, the normal relationship of lovers. In a poetry relentlessly metaphysical, it is part of Salinas's achievement that he maintains a distance and objectivity in his overheard confession. In fact, with a prosy exactitude and extravagant imagination, he takes the simplest acts of the love experience, gives them importance, and conveys joy or pathos.

Salinas's poem has a Cervantine, oxymoronic optimism-pessimism throughout. We know, or suspect, even from the beginning, that there will be a failure. There is too much joy for it to be otherwise. No matter. He will stick with the reality of felicity, of the pink naked body, the laughter and the tenderness, the barbed words and the disappearance; for all that is real. Time can only alter tenses, not change the facts of the love's reality. The existence of the poem, preserving and reliving the love, proves the persistence of the love.

But there is a movement in the poem toward darkness, and this must be acknowledged. By an act of will, when loss appears certain, the persona keeps inventing and reinventing the woman. Even the sorrow becomes tangible proof of her existence:

> In that drowned
> reality that denies
> itself and claims
> it never was,
> that it was only my
> pretext for living.
> If you did not stick with me,
> irrefutable sorrow,
> I might agree.
> But you stay.
> Your truth assures me
> that nothing was a lie.

He remembers that when she "chose" him, he "came out of the great anonymity." And when

> . . . you said "you"
> to me, yes, to me singled out—
> I was higher than stars,
> deeper than coral.
> And my joy
> began to spin, caught
> in your being, in your pulse.

> You gave me possession of
>   myself
> when you gave your self to
>   me.
> I lived. I live. How long?
> I know you will back out.

When it is over, Salinas recognizes how the holocaust will be:

> When you go
> I will go back to a deaf
> world that does not
>   distinguish
> gram or drop
> in weight or water.
> I'll be one more—like the
>   rest—
> when you are lost.
> I'll lose my name,
> my age, my gestures, all
> lost in me, from me.
> Gone back to the immense
>   bone heap
> of those who have not died
> and now have no death to die
> in life.

He lives now with disappearance, memory, shadows he tries to grab, and awakens a second time, shaking. He lives with impossibility. It is not simply the loss of love—Antonio Machado tells us that love is in the absence—and Salinas recognizes ordinary separation. But it is the impossibility of leaving the circle, the trap, for whatever unstated reason, that raises the sequence of poems from simple sadness to a dimension of common tragedy. Man is trapped and fated to live a few seconds, invent, remember, and lose the outside as he will ultimately lose his own consciousness to senility or death. As the poems progress, the loss of so much beauty and love is expressed as a precise, unbearable fact. He relieves the "starving dream" by evocation of earlier wonder. And there is only one poem, number 61, in which he slips into total weakness, acknowledging desolation and asking that it be shared by the lover. This embarrassment, sentimentality if you will, somehow authenticates both the experience itself and the fullness and artistry of the surrounding poems. He does not willfully conceal his human frailty by self-conscious art:

And quiet,
with that quietness
of light and knowledge,
you would kiss me more,
desolately,
with a desolation
that has no other being or
    pain
beside it—one alone
with pain—
trying to help some other
chimera's
sorrow.

Salinas brings to his love sequence many kinds of dexterity.
Psychologically, there is perhaps no modern poet—and he is
above all a poet who has neither aged nor thinned in importance—who so subtly and rigorously uses external data, fil-
tered and clarified in internal consciousness, to give the reader
an objective account of the physical and emotional life of man
and woman. He is a poet of rigorous intelligence, who enjoys
playing with ideas, humorously, ironically, and with an un-
imaginably detailed persistence. His metaphors often extend
into multiple surfaces and qualifications, yet clarity prevails.
Indeed his elaborations are curiously misleading, for while
they appear to be ingeniously fitted together, they also have
the directness and flow of Molly Bloom's soliloquy, and what
at first glance appears complex is the complexity of direct, if
elliptical, candor.

The chaos, images, passions, pathos of that mind are pres-
ented in seventy linked cumulatively powerful meditations.
Salinas photographs the mind—going down very deep, as
far as the lens of language can see.

The poetry of Pedro Salinas lends itself to modern trans-
lation and more so than that of most of his contemporaries.
Obviously this English version was done because of the value
of the poem. But I should also acknowledge that I am repaying
a debt to Pedro Salinas and his family. As an undergraduate
I had the good luck to hear Pedro Salinas lecture in the Spanish
School at Middlebury College. Later I spent a week in the
Salinas house in Baltimore, visiting the poet's son, Jaime
Salinas, who at that time first opened the Spanish world to
me. Professor Juan Marichal at Harvard, editor of the first

Poesías completas, has always given much appreciated encouragement, and his wife, Solita, daughter of Pedro Salinas and editor of the 1971 text used for this translation, has been extraordinarily helpful. She went over each poem meticulously and saved the manuscript, not from unwarranted poetic freedoms but from many, many mistakes of interpretation of Pedro Salinas's subtly composed poems. Finally, Jorge Guillén, the great Spanish poet, has once again written about his friend Pedro Salinas, as he must know Salinas would be doing for him, were he alive today. When I asked don Jorge for some introductory pages, his answer was true to his affirmative *Cántico* and *sí: "Si no tuviera ganas, lo haría . . . ."* "If I did not feel like doing it, I would do it, and since I very much want to, you will have it in a month." My thanks to all.

Willis Barnstone

A Note on the Poet

Pedro Salinas (1891-1951) was born in Madrid and, like his lifelong friend Jorge Guillén, was a poet, a professor, and an excellent scholar and critic. After teaching at the University of Seville, the Sorbonne, and at several other European universities, he came to the United States in 1936 where he taught at Wellesley College. The last years of his life were spent at the Johns Hopkins University. He died in Boston in 1951.

His collected poems, *Poesías completas*, with a prologue by Jorge Guillén, appeared in Barcelona in 1971 (Barral Editores), edited by his daughter, Soledad Salinas de Marichal. This edition includes nine volumes of poems, plus some early and late poems: *Presagios*, 1923; *Seguro azar*, 1929; *Fábula y signo*, 1931; *La voz a ti debida; 1933, Razón de amor*, 1936; *Largo lamento*, 1936-38 (this third book of the love trilogy appears in its entirety only in the *Poesías completas* of 1975); *El contemplado*, 1946; *Todo más claro*, 1949; *Confianza*, 1955.

In addition, Salinas wrote prose sketches in *Víspera del gozo*, 1926; a novel, *La bomba increíble*, 1950; a collection of short stories, *El desnudo impecable y otras narraciones*, 1951. His collected plays were edited by Juan Marichal in *Teatro completo*, 1957.

He did many critical editions, put the epic poem *Cantar de Mio Cid* into modern Spanish, and wrote seven volumes of essays and literary criticism: *Reality and Poet in Spanish Poetry*, 1940; *Literatura española siglo XX*, 1949; *La poesía de Rubén Darío*, 1946; *Jorge Manrique, o tradición y originalidad*, 1949; *El defensor*, 1948; *Ensayos de literatura hispánica*, 1958; and *La responsibilidad del escritor y otros ensayos*, 1961.

MY VOICE BECAUSE OF YOU

Thou Wonder, and thou Beauty, and thou Terror
Shelley, *Epipsychidion*

1

You live always in your acts.
With the tip of your fingers
you play the world, you root out
dawns and triumphs and colors,
joys: it is your music.
Life is what you touch.

From your eyes, only from them,
comes a light that guides
footsteps. You walk
where you see. Nothing else.

And if a doubt alerts you
from ten thousand miles away,
you drop everything, you rush
onto prows, upon wings,
you are already there; with kisses,
with your teeth you rip it out:
no longer a doubt.
You can never doubt.

For you have turned mysteries
inside out. And your enigmas
(that you'll never understand)
are those clearest things:
the sand where you lie down,
the ticking of your watch
and the tender pink body
that you meet in the mirror
every day in waking,
and it's yours. Prodigies, marvels
that are now deciphered.

And you were never wrong.
Only once. One night when
you fell in love with a shadow
(the only one you cared for).
It seemed a shadow.
And you wanted to hug it.
And it was me.

2

No, don't lock up
the gates of the night,
the wind, lightning,
what has never been seen.
Let the known ones always
be open.
And all the unknown doors,
opening
onto long roads,
stubborn, dark
highways in the wind
that seek their way
and find nothing,
no cardinal points.
Hang up high signs,
wonders, stars;
let it be clearly seen
that here everything
wants to receive her.
She can come.
Today or tomorrow, or in
a thousand years, or on the next-
to-last-day of the world.
And all must be as smooth
as the long wait.

Though I know it is useless.
That it's a game,
waiting for her
as for a breath or breeze,
afraid she may stumble.
For when she comes

unleashed and implacable
to reach me,
walls, names, seasons
will shatter,
come apart, pierced
irresistibly
by the huge sea gale
of her love. Now a presence.

3

Yes, behind other people
I look for you.
Not in your name if they say it,
not in your image if they paint it.
Behind, behind, beyond.

In back of you I look for you.
Not in your mirror, not in your letter,
not in your soul.
Behind, beyond.

Behind and even further
I look for you. You are not
what I feel you.
You are not
what is quivering
in veins with my blood
without being me.
I look for you behind, beyond.

To live finally behind it all,
on the other side of it all
—to find you—
as if it were dying.
To find you, I stop
living in you, and in me,
and in the others.

4

If you called me, yes,
if you called me!

I would drop everything,
toss it all away:
costs, catalogues,
blue on the ocean maps,
days and their nights,
old telegrams
and a love.
You, who are not my love,
if you called me!

And I still wait for your voice:
telescopes down below,
from a star,
through mirrors, through tunnels,
leap years.
It might come. I don't know which way.
Always from some wonder.
For if you call me
if you called me, yes, if you called me!—
it will be from a miracle, unknown,
unseen.

Never from your lips I kiss,
never
from your voice that says: "Don't go."

5

It was, it happened, it's true.
On a day, a calendar date
that stamps time upon time.
It was in a place I see.
Her feet walked on the floor,
the one we all walk upon.
Her dress
looked like the others
women wear.
Her watch
took the calendar apart
without missing an hour,
as they say.
And what she told me
was in a worldly tongue,
with grammar and history.
So true
it looked like a lie.

No.
I must live it inside,
and have to dream it out.
Get rid of the color, number,
the breath of pure fire
that scorched me when she said it.
Must turn it into accident,
pure chance, dreaming it out.
And so when she takes back
what she told me then,
the pain won't mawl me
for having lost a joy

I had in my arms—the same
as holding a body.
I will think I was dreaming.
That this thing, so true,
had no body or name.
That I lose
a shadow, one more dream.

6

Fear. Of you. Loving you
is the very highest risk.
Multiples, you and your life.
I have you, your life today;
I know it now, go inside
through labyrinths, easy
thanks to you, to your hand.
And now they are mine, yes.
But you are
your own beyond,
like light and the world:
days, nights, summers,
winters in a row.
You change inescapably
and never stop being you
in your own transformation,
with constant
fidelity to change.

Tell me, will I live
in those other climates
or futures or lights
that you are elaborating
for your tomorrow
as the fruit ripens its juice?
Or will I be only
something born for one day
yours (my eternal day),
for one spring
(flowering in me always),
and not able to live

when inevitably
come
successive forces and new
winds, other fires
now waiting for the moment
to be, in you, your life?

7

"Tomorrow." The word
was loose, vacant,
feathery in the wind,
so soulless and bodyless,
so missing color or kiss,
that I let it slip
by me, in my today.
But suddenly you
said: "Tomorrow, I . . . ."
And all was peopled
with flesh and banners.
Then promises
in six hundred colors
fell on top of me.
They were elegant,
naked, but all
charged with tenderness.
They came to me in trains
or on gazelles—sharp
violin sounds—
delicate hopes
of virgin mouths.
Or swift and great
like ships, far
like whales
from remote seas,
immense hopes
of an endless love.
Tomorrow! What a wholly
vibrating word, tense
with soul and rose flesh,
a bowstring where

you placed the sharpest
weapon of twenty years,
a relentless arrow
when you said: "I . . . ."

8

And suddenly, at once,
yes, joy.
Alone—that's how she wanted
it—she came. So vertical,
such unhoped for grace,
a gift fallen from nowhere,
that I can't believe
it's for me.
I look around,
I search. Whose could it be?
Can it be that island
escaped from the map,
that passed near me
dressed like a girl,
with sea foam on her neck,
green dress and a big
sprinkling of adventures?
Won't it fall this way
on a third, a ninth, a fifth
of now in August?
Or is it what I saw quivering
behind a hope,
in the depths of a voice
that was telling me: "No."?

But it doesn't matter now.
She is with me. She drags me,
tears me out of doubt.
She smiles, possible;
it takes the form of kisses,
of arms toward me;

she looks mine.
I will go, I will go with her
so we can love, can live
trembling with future,
to feel her quickly,
seconds, centuries, forevers,
nothings. And I will love her
so much that when someone
comes
— and he will come unseen,
his steps will be
unheard—to ask me for her
(it is her master, she was his),
when they carry her off,
docile, to her place, she
will turn her head
looking at me. And I will see
that now yes she is mine, now.

9

Why do you have a name:
day, Wednesday?
Why do you have a name:
time, autumn?
Happiness, pain, always,
why do you have a name—love?

If you had no name
I would not know what it was,
or how or when. Nothing.

Does the sea know its name,
that it's the sea? Do winds know
their nominations, South Wind,
North Wind, beyond
the simple heaving breath they are?

If you had no name,
all would be primary,
a beginning, all invented
by me,
intact until my kiss.
Pleasure, love: slow delight
of enjoying, loving, nameless.

Name, what a knife stuck
in the middle of a naked chest,
ours always,
were it not for its name!

10

How many lost things
that were never lost!
You kept them all.

Minute seeds of time
the wind carried off one day.
Alphabets of foam
the sea carried off one day.
I gave them up for lost.

And the clouds I wanted
to control
in the sky
nailing them with gazes. Lost too.
And tall joys
of loving, and pangs
of still caring little,
and the hunger
to love, to love you more.
All lost, all
a thing that was before,
now never to be.

And then out of darkness
you came, luminous
in young deep patience,
lightly, so the past
that brought you so young
to me, would not weigh
on your slender waist,
your naked shoulders.

When I saw you in the virgin
kisses you gave me,
the spume and seasons,
clouds and loves I lost
were saved.
If they escaped from me,
it was not to go die
in oblivion.
They were living in you.
What I called forgetting
was you.

11

There, behind laughter
no one knows you now.
You go and come, slide
through a world of frozen
waltzes, downhill;
and as you wander, whims
and impulses snatch
uninvolved kisses
from you, a momentary
captive of easiness.
"How happy she is!" they all say.
And now you want
to be another you,
resembling you so much
I am afraid
of losing you. Like that.

I pursue you. I wait, know
when tunnels and planets
don't look at you,
when people think they
know who you are
and say: "Yes, now I know,"
and with your arms high
you will undo
the knot back of
your hair, and look at me.
With no noise of breaking glass
your laughter,
now a useless
airy mask,

will topple to the floor.
And when you see yourself in
the love I always give you
like a flaming mirror,
you will recognize
a grave grave face
of a stranger,
tall, pallid and sad,
that is my darling. And she
loves me behind her laughter.

12

I don't need time
to know what you're like:
knowing is lightning.
Who can know you in
what you silence, in those
words you stifle?
If one seeks you in the life
you live, one has only
allusions to you,
pretexts where you hide.
To follow you back into
what you have done before,
is to tie action with smile,
years with names, and to go on
losing you. Not me.
I met you in the storm.
I knew you suddenly
in that brutal
breaking out of gloom and light,
where the bottom is revealed
that escapes day and darkness.
I saw you, you saw me, and now
stripped naked of error,
of history, of past,
you are an amazon in the flashing
sky, throbbing as a recent
unhoped for arrival,
you are so anciently mine,
I know you so long
that I shut my eyes in your love
and walk arrow straight,

blind, asking nothing,
into the slow certain light
where letters
and forms are added up
and I think I see
who you are: my invisible being.

13

What an enormous first night!
The world! Nothing was made.
No matter, no numbers,
no stars, no centuries. Nothing.
Coal was not black
nor the rose tender.
Nothing was still nothing.
How innocent to believe
that the past of others
in another time was
forever irrevocable!
No, the past was ours:
it had no name.
We could call it
anything we liked: galaxy,
humming bird, theorem
instead of "past";
to get the poison out.
A huge wind blew
continents, mines,
motors toward us.
What kind of mines? Empty.
They were waiting for
our first desire,
to fill up suddenly
with copper, with poppies.
Cities, ports
floated over the world
with no place yet:
they were waiting for
you to say: "Here,"
before spilling out ships,

machines, parties.
Impatient machines
with no purpose yet;
for they would make light
if you ordered it,
or autumn nights
if you wanted them.
Indecisive verbs
looked at your eyes
like faithful dogs,
tremulous. Your command
would finally trace out
their routes, actions.
Climb up? Their ignorant
energy was quivering.
Would climbing mean
going up? And where
would going down be?
With messages to the poles,
to day stars, your order
made them
abruptly aware of being,
to fly or creep over the earth.
The great empty world
was inert
before you: you would give it
its push.
And next to you, hollow
from new birth, on the edge,
with my eyes shut,
preparing my body
for pain and the kiss,
with blood in place,
I was waiting
—O what if you did not see me!—
for you to want me
and to say: "Now."

14

To live I don't want
islands, palaces, towers.
What steeper joy
than living in pronouns!

Take off your clothing,
features, pictures;
I don't want you like that,
masked as another,
always a daughter of something.
I want you pure, free,
irreducible: you.
I know when I call you
among all people
in the world,
only you will be you.
And when you ask me
who is calling you,
who wants you his,
I will bury nouns,
labels, history.
I will tear apart
all they threw on me
before I was born.
And finally back in the eternal
anonymity of nakedness,
of stone, of the world,
I will tell you:
"I love you, yes. I'm the one."

15

Happiness quickly,
rushed, crazy.
She is drunk and shot out
casually from a bow
against the sky and earth.
Physics is astonished
and fearful; trains
stay even further
behind than airplanes
and light. It is she,
at top velocity, blind
with gazing, seeing nothing,
and wanting what she sees.
And no longer wants it.
For she has slipped out
of wanting, of desire
and fully drunk in its essence,
she asks nothing, goes
nowhere, ignores
horns, shouts,
threats. She flattens
patience and the world
with her light feet.
And she pours ruin on
order, time, sorrows,
in a total triumphant
abolition of all
that is not she: candid
joy, tallest joy
looming
on top of itself.

She strives so high
that now she is falling,
doubled up like a hero
on her futile deed.
And now she is dying
consumed, undone
by the air, a perfect
combustion of her being.
And she won't leave smoke,
corpse or grief behind—
a memory of having been.
And no one will know, no one,
for she alone
found out in herself. And died.

16

Everything says yes.
Yes from the sky, blueness,
and yes blue from the sea,
oceans, skies, blues
in sea foam and breezes
repeat jubilant
monosyllables endlessly.
A yes answers yes
to another yes. Great repeated
dialogues are heard
above the sea
from world to world: yes.
Long yeses read
in the wind, lightning rays
of stock feathers
so snowy they fall
flake by flake covering
the earth in an enormous
white yes. It is the great day.
Today we can go close
to what does not talk:
to the cliff, to love,
the bone behind the forehead.
They are slaves of yes.
It is the only word
the world concedes them.
Soul, quickly ask
for a maximum
momentary madness,
ask for impossible
things asked for

so long and so many times
in silence
and that today we will shout!
Certain for one day
—today, only today—
that the no's were false,
simply appearances, delays,
innocent coverings.
And behind,
slowly ripening,
in measure with the hunger
of asking hopelessly
for rapture: the yes.

17

Love, love, catastrophe.
What a foundering world!
A deep horror of roofs
cracks columns and seasons;
replaces them with non-
temporal heavens. You walk, I walk
through the debris
of summers and collapsed
winters. Measures and weights
are wiped out. All
life spins backward,
frantically tossing off
centuries; it tears loose
galloping
down the once slow track;
crazy to erase
history,
to be no more than pure
thirst to begin
again. The future
is called yesterday. Yesterday
occult and secret
that we forgot
and must win again
with blood and soul,
behind the other known
yesterdays.
Behind, always back there!
Dizzy regressions
inwardly toward tomorrow!
Let it all collapse! I

hardly care. Strong
in our kisses, let us
invent the ruins
of the world, hand in hand,
you and I
through the great failure
of flowers and order.
And now I feel your flesh,
between touching and hugs,
that sends me
back to our first vibrations:
dark, before the world began,
total, unformed, chaos.

18

What a sinless day!
Foam, hour after hour,
untiringly
white, white, white.
Bodies and rocks,
innocent matter
—all the way from zenith
absolute noon—
were
living from the light
and through the light and in her.·
Awareness and shadow
were still unknown.
A hand reached out
to pick up a stone,
a cloud, a flower,
a wing.
And it reached everywhere
because it came
before there were distances.
Time had no suspicion
of being itself.
It came to us
submissive and flexible.
To live slowly,
quickly, we were saying,
"Stop" or "Start to run."
To live, live,
nothing else, you were saying,
"Go."
And so it left us
floating weightless

in pure living
with no afterward,
safe from motives,
from origins and dawns.
That day, you and I
had no idea how
to turn our heads or
look far. We did not need
to. To kiss, yes.
But with lips
so far from their cause
that they saw everything new,
kiss, love, in the flash of kissing,
and had to beg
pardon from no one, nothing.

19

Yes, everything, in excess:
light, life, the sea!
All plural, plural,
lights, lives and seas.
To climb, to ascend
from dozens to hundreds,
from hundreds to a thousand,
in a delicious
interminable repetition
of your love, a unity.
Tables, pens, and machines
are just for multiplying
caress by caress,
embrace by volcano.
We must wear out the numbers.
Let them count endlessly,
get drunk counting
so they won't know
what will be last:
Life with no ending!
Let a great flock of zeros
assault our thin
joys, and take them, as they go,
to their peak.
Let ciphers burst
and foul the calculation
of time and kisses.
And beyond
computations, destinies,
deliver us blind
—what a penultimate excess!—

to a vast risky depth
that irresistibly
is
singing to us in fulgent
shouts of the future:
"This is nothing yet.
Look deeply at your selves. There's more."

20

Lovers
wanderingly through the world.
To love! What unequaled
confusion! How many errors!
To kiss faces
rather than the masks we love.
A jumbled universe:
minerals in flower
sailing through the sky,
sirens and coral
in perpetual snow,
and on the sea floor
constellations
tired now, fugitives
in the great orphan night
where divers die.
The two of us. What disasters!
Where's the road? Here,
there? False maps,
juggling the routes,
gamble for our loss
among beaconless dangers.
Days and kisses
walk mixed up:
they don't end where they say.
But to love
we must ship out on all
passing projects,
asking nothing,
filled big with faith
in the mistake
of yesterday, today, tomorrow

that has to be.
With cleanest joy
of not guessing right, not finding
ourselves on doorsills, on
shaky borders of victory,
not caring to win.
With the unique felicity
of living a life
innocent among errors,
wanting only
to be, to love, to love each other
in the great altitude
of a love that is now
working
so detached
from what is not itself
that it looms
over triumphs or defeats,
drunk in the pure
glory of coming out right.

21

What joy, to live
feeling I am living through her.
To surrender
darkly to the great certainty
that another being, outside me, remote,
is living me. For when mirrors, spies
—quicksilver, dwarfed souls—prove
that I am here, me, motionless,
with eyes shut and lips,
denying myself love
of light, of a flower and of names,
I walk through a transparent truth
without my footsteps, with others,
remote, and there
I kiss flowers, lights, I talk.
There is another being through whom I see the world
because she loves me with her eyes.
There is another voice I say things through,
unsuspected by my great silence;
and she also loves me with her voice.
Life—what transcendency!—ignorance
of what my acts are, and hers,
in which she lives, a double, hers and mine.
And when she tells me
about a dark sky, a white landscape
I will remember
stars I did not see, that she was looking at,
and snow that snowed up there in her sky.
With the strange thrill of remembering
how I touched what I did not touch

except with hands that I can't reach
with my distant hands.
And entirely carried away, my body
will be able to rest, quiet, dead. And die
in deep confidence
that my living was not only
my living: it was ours. And another being
lives me behind the no death.

22

Labor
not to let your beauty
keep me apart from you.

Flight
for not staying where you want:
here, in the alphabets,
in daybreaks, in lips.

Thirst
to slowly leave behind
anecdotes, clothing and caresses;
to reach
through all
that is changing in you
to nakedness and permanence.

And while
your faces, whims and kisses,
your mercurial delights, your quick
contacts with the world
spin round and round, giving in,
getting fooled,
to have come
to the pure unmoving center in you
and to see how you change
— you call it living —
in everything, yes in everything
except in me where you survive.

23

I can't give you more.
I am no more than I am.

O how I would like to be
sand, sun, of summer!
So you might lie down
refreshed, to relax.
So when you go you might leave me
your body as a tender
warm unforgettable imprint.
And that my slow kiss might be
upon you:
color
from nape to heels,
a darkness.

O how I would like to be
glass or quilt or wood
that keeps its color
here, its aroma here,
though born three thousand miles away.

To be
the material you like,
that you touch every day
and see without looking
around
—necklace, flask, ancient silk—
things that when you miss
you say: "O where is that?"

And O how I would like to be
the one happiness of all,
the one
that makes you happy!
One love, one love:
the love you might fall in love with.

But
I am no more than I am.

24

Wake up. Day calls you
to your life: your duty.
And to live, nothing else.
Root it out of the glum
night and the shadow
that covered your body
for which light waits
on tiptoe in the dawn.
Stand up, affirm the straight
simple will to be
a pure vertical virgin.
Test your body's metal.
Cold, heat? Your blood
will say it against the snow,
behind the window.
The color
in your cheeks will say it.
And look at the world. Rest
doing no more than adding
your perfection to another day.
Your task
is to carry your life high,
play with it, hurl it
like a voice to the clouds
so it may retrieve the lights
already gone from us.
That is your fate: to live.
Do nothing.
Your work is you, nothing else.

25

The trouble with light
is it doesn't come from you.
It comes from suns,
from rivers, from the olive.
I love your darkness more.

Happiness
is never the same hand
that gives it. Today it's one,
tomorrow, yesterday another.
But never yours.
That's why I always take
sorrow from you, what you give me.
Telegraph wires carry
kisses, touch
in dense nights,
future lips.
They come from where they come.
I don't feel the kiss.

And that's why I don't want it,
or want to owe it
to I don't know whom.
To you
I'd like to owe it all.
What a handsome world, how sound
if all kisses and light
I enjoy
came only from you!

26

A present or a gift?
Pure symbol, signal
that I want to give myself.
What pain to be separate
from what I send you
and what belongs to you
with only the end
of being yours, your own,
while I remain
on the other bank alone,
still mine.
How I would like to be
what I give you
and not the one who gives it.
When I tell you:
"I am yours, only yours,"
I am afraid of a cloud,
a city, a number
that can rob me
of a minute from the full
love I owe you.
Ah! if I were the rose
I give you; that was in danger
of being something else
and not for your hands,
before I came.
Since it will now have
no future but to be
my rose in your rose,
lived in you, by you,
in its smell, touch.

Until you raise it
above its wilting
to become a memory of a safe
rose, unfadeable,
secure
from another love or life
you might be living.

27

Sleep is a long
going from you.
What a great life with you,
tall and sharp in dream!
Let the world sleep, the sun,
ants, hours,
all, every sleeping thing,
sleep in the dream I sleep.
Except you, alone,
alive, surviving
in the dream I dream.

But yes, a goodbye:
I will leave you. Soon
the morning prepares
its full precision
of sunrays and laughters.
Out with the dream
floating
hovering above the world,
unable to touch it
—it has no place to be—
desperately!

I hug you for the last time.
It opens our eyes.
That's it. Verticals
come in to work
without faltering. In order.
Colors exercise
their office of blueness,

of pink, green, all
right on time. The world
will function well
today: it killed the dream.
I feel you flee from dawn,
easy, and travel
exactly upward, seeking
the unseen star,
celestial disorder,
the only place you can be.
Then, when I wake up,
I don't know you, almost,
when by my side you stretch
your arms to me
saying: "What were you dreaming?"
And I would answer: "I don't know,
I forgot,"
if your clean
exact body were not already
offering me in its lips
the great error of daylight.

28

What circles your wrist
of time against time!
A watch, cold, coiled up,
spying, waits for
the passage of blood
in your pulse. Outside
orders crush you:
tick tick, tick tick,
the voice there in the machine.
The seconds throw puerile
lassos upon
your stopless infinite life.
But your heart
far off
—blood coming and going
in you, with your love—
affirms its being, rhythm, as something
else. No. Your days, your time,
will never be counted
on white dials
as three, four, five, six.
Your laziness, whims,
great uncalculated fervor,
can't be coded.
Feel them naked
of the watch on your wrist:
a throbbing against number.
Love? Living? Hear
the diminutive tick tick
that twenty years ago
sounded first

in flesh virgin
to the touch of light,
to carry to the world
a distinct calculation,
singular, new: you.

29

When you close your eyes
your eyelids are wind.
They stir me:
to go to you, inside.

Nothing is seen, nothing
is heard. Eyes and lips
are my abundance
in your world.
To feel you
the usual senses
used on others
don't work.
We must wait for new ones.
I walk at your side
deafly in darkness,
tripping over chance,
on the brink; sinking
to the top
with a great weight of wings.

When you open
your eyes I turn
to the outside, now blind,
and stumble,
unable to see a thing
here.
Not knowing how to live
in the other, in yours,
or in this discolored world
where I was living.

I am nothing
between the two.
I go, come
from one to the other
when you want me to,
when you open, close
your eyelids, your eyes.

30

Yes, I want you horizontal.
Look at the face of the sky
face up. Enough
worry about balance
where you and I weep.
Give yourself
to the great final truth,
of what you will be with me,
stretched out, parallel,
in death or in a kiss.
Night is horizontal
on the sea, a great shuddering mass
over the sleeping earth,
vanquished on the beach.
Standing up is a lie:
only racing or lying down.
And what you and I want
and also the day—so tired
of being upright in light—
is to be reached, alive
and with a trembling of death
at the summit of our kiss,
to be exhausted
by the most unweighted love,
its weight coming from earth,
things, earth's flesh.
In the night and beyond night
and love and beyond love,
you and I
are changed from ourselves
into final horizons.

31

Push me, drive me away
from you, your cheeks,
as from islands of coral,
to sail far off
to find you, to find
outside you what you have,
what you don't want to give me.

To remain alone,
invent virgin forests
with trees of metal
and jet; I will go to them
and see that they were only
necklaces in your thoughts.
Invite me to splendors
and sparkle: far,
black, white, smiling
of childhood. I'll look for them.
I'll walk days and days
and when I get there
I'll find your wide
laughter, your bright gaze.

That
is what way over there
I saw shining.

From so much voyage
don't expect me to bring you
more worlds, more springs
than these—your defense
against me. Going and coming

to centuries, mines,
dreams, is hopeless.
I always come out of you, always
must return to you.

32

I can no longer find you
there in that distance, with its precise name,
where you were missing.
Coming to find me
you abandoned it. You came out of your absence,
and yet I don't see you or know where you are.
I would go futilely to find you,
where my thought went so often
to catch your dream or your laughter or your game.
No longer there. You took them away;
away to bring them to me,
but you still wander
between here and there. You hold my soul
hanging over a great emptiness,
unable to kiss your certain body
that is about to come back;
and your missing form also ran off
and has not yet returned from the known absence
where we used to meet, dreaming.
Your only life is wanting to come.
You live in transit, in coming toward me,
but not on the sea, on the earth, in the air
which you cross anxiously with your body
as if you were traveling.
And lost, blind,
I don't know what to reach you with, where you are,
if just in opening a door
or shouting will work; or if you will only
hear, feel me, my hunger will reach you
in its absolute motionless waiting
for love, imminence, joy, panic,
with only the wings of silence, wings.

33

No, they don't love you, no.
Yes you are loving.

The extra love you have
is shared by beings
and things you look at,
touch, that never
had love before.
When you say: "Tigers
or shadows love me"
it means you were in forests
or nights promenading
your great thirst to love.
You're no good as the loved one;
you will always win, caring more
than one who cares for you.
A lover, not the loved one.
And what I might give you,
broken, here, adoring you,
you give yourself:
your implacable love
no possible equal,
that returns to itself
through my
body, now overwhelmed
by endless memory,
never a forgetting,
that once let you pass through it
—I still feel the fire—
blind to your destiny.
So that one fine day
you came
to your love through my love.

34

What you are
distracts me from what you say.

Quick words tossed out,
with sails of laughter,
inviting me
to go where they take me.
I don't pay attention or trace them out:
I am looking at
the lips where they were born.

Suddenly you look far off.
You nail your glance there,
I don't know on what, and your soul
shoots out to find it,
sharpened like an arrow.
I don't look where you look:
I see your gaze.

And when you want something
I don't think of what you want,
nor am I jealous; that's the least.
You want it today, you desire it,
tomorrow you will forget
through some new love.
No. I wait for you beyond
endings and boundaries.
In what cannot happen
I hang on. In the pure act
of your desire. Wanting you.
I care for nothing else
but to see you wanting.

35

The skies are the same.
Blues, grays, blacks,
repeated above
the orange tree or the stone:
looking at them draws us near.
Being so far away
stars rub out
the world's distances.
If we want to come close,
never look ahead:
all those chasms,
dates and miles.
Better to float
on sea or grass,
still, face to the sky.
You will feel yourself plunge
down slowly upward
into the life of air.
And we will meet
above the unconquerable
differences, sands,
rocks, years, now alone,
celestial swimmers,
shipwrecked from the heavens.

36

Yesterday I kissed you on the lips.
I kissed you on the lips. Dense,
red. It was such a quick kiss
that it lasted longer than lightning,
than a miracle, longer.
Time
—after giving you this—
was nothing
to me, I had wanted it
for nothing before.
It began and ended in the flash.

Today I kiss a kiss;
I am alone with my lips.
I put them
not in your mouth, no not now
—where did it get away to?—
I put them
in the kiss I gave you
yesterday, in our joined mouths
of the kiss they kissed.

And this kiss lasts longer
than silence, than light.
For it is no longer flesh
or a mouth I kiss.
That slips away, escapes from me.
No.
I am kissing you further away.

37

What you have given me
should be enough.
And I ask for more, more.
Each shade of your beauty
is to me the extreme
fulfillment of yourself:
you will never be able to give
anything more perfect
from yourself. My eyes
close now, missionless,
in overflowing light.
As you gave it to me
life is complete:
you are at the end.

And suddenly I feel—
as you were entering
your own elevation from
yourself—you are reborn.
In your end you begin
again. And the gift
of your loveliness
opens
—clean, a surprise—
new beauty:
like the first.
Because your surrender is
a reconquest
turned inward, an increase.
So
to ask you to love me

is to ask it for you;
is to say to you to live,
to go
even beyond
ultimate
mines of your being.
The life I implore
you to have inexhaustible,
I illuminate by asking you.
And I won't end it
however much I ask it to be
infinite. No.
I yes I will come to an end,
while you, generous,
renew yourself and live
again you, expanded
in your endless gifts.

38

How totally the stone falls!
Nothing in it dissents
from its destiny, from its law: the ground.
Don't explain your love to yourself or to me;
to obey it is enough. Block out
your eyes and questions. Sink
into your desire, a law preceding
will. And fill
that other plunge that waits behind
fatal death
with yeses, banners, joys. Better not to love
looking at each other complacent mirrors,
undoing
that great unity with doomed tricks;
better for us not to love
with wings in the atmosphere,
like butterflies or clouds,
floating. Look for weights,
the deepest in you, so they can drag you down
to the great center where I wait for you.
Total love, wanting each other like masses.

39

The form of your loving
is to let me love you.
The yes with which you yield to me
is silence. Your kisses
are an offering of lips
so I can kiss them.
Never words or arms
will tell me you existed,
loved me: never.
Blank pages tell me,
maps, auguries, telephones;
not you.
I hold you
not asking you, out of fear
it may be untrue
that you live and want me.
I hold you
without looking and touching you.
Fearing to reveal
with questions or caressing
the immense solitude
of me alone wanting you.

40

How probable you are!
If my eyes tell me
(as I look at you) no,
that you are not real,
then hands and lips
with my eyes closed
run through delicate
proofs: the slow
conviction of your being rises
by the ladder of touch,
mouths, flesh and flesh.
If I still don't believe,
then something more solid,
palpable, the voice
with which you say: "I love you"
fights to affirm yourself
against my doubts. Next to me
a body kisses, embraces
frenetically, seeking
its reality here
in me: that I don't believe;
it kisses
to make its still indecisive
life
a pure miracle, in me.
And slowly you form
yourself,
being born
inside your desire,
my desire, confused,
as day is formed

in a great dark doubt.
And the former doubting
creature that you leave
behind is in agony,
a worthless being of the past,
so that the irrefutable you
can finally leap out;
a naked certain Venus
between definite dawns,
who wins her new being from herself,
wanting me.

41

Forgive me for seeking you this way
so clumsily inside
you,
forgive the hurting, at times.
It's that I want to take out
of you the best you.
That you did not see and I see:
a swimmer through your delicious sea depths.
And to seize it
and hold it up
as a tree holds the last light
it found in the sun.
And then you
in your searching would come to the top.
To get there
you rise over your self the way I want you,
barely touching your past
with the pink edge of your feet,
your whole body tense, ascending
from you to your self.

And then let my love be answered
in the new creature you were.

42

How long have we been talking?
Who began it? I don't know.
My questions are the days;
your obscure, broad, vague
answers, the nights.
When they join
they form the world, time,
for you and for me.
My question drops
into the light of nothing,
hushed
so you can answer
with erroneous stars;
then, newly born
at dawn, astonished
by the young hunger
of asking the same things
as yesterday,
that the night answered
halfway, bursting with stars.
Years and life,
what an anguished dialogue!
Nevertheless,
almost everything is still unsaid.
And when we separate
and cannot hear each other
I will keep telling you:
"How quickly it collapsed!
And we had so much to say, so much
left in us to say!"

43

The questions start
flaming at night.
Distant, quiet,
enormous like planets:
and from out there they always
ask
the same: how can you be?
Other tiny evasive ones
would like to know
gay and exact things:
your shoe
size, the name
of the street in the world
where you would wait for me.

You can't see them
but keep the dream
surrounded
by my
interrogations.
And maybe once,
dreaming, you will say
yes and no, random
and miraculous answers
to questions you don't know,
don't see or understand.
For you know nothing;
and when you wake up
they hide, invisible,
extinguished.
And you will go on living
happy,

not knowing that in half your life
you are always circled
by worry, efforts, longing,
endless questions
you don't see
or can't answer.

44

What a night walk
with your absence at my side!
My companion is the feeling
of your not coming with me.
Mirrors, water
believe I go alone;
eyes believe it.
Sirens out of the sky
still spurting stars,
slender languid girls
who step out of cars
call me. I don't hear them.
I still have your voice
in my ear when you said:
"Don't go." And those,
your two last words,
are talking to me
endlessly, and answer
what my life asked
the first day.
Phantoms, shadows, dreams,
past loves,
taking pity,
want to come along,
to offer a hand.
But immediately they see
I keep the form of a hand
squeezed, warm, live, tender,
quivering in mine.
That you handed me
when you said: "Don't go."

They go, they leave,
phantoms, shadows,
dumbfounded
to see they don't leave me alone.
And then deep night,
darkness, cold,
also fooled,
come to kiss me.
They can't; another kiss
comes between my lips.
It does not go away,
it won't leave. The one you gave me,
looking at my eyes
when I left,
saying: "Don't go."

45

Matter has no weight.
Neither your body nor mine
joined ever feels
serfdom. Wings yes.
Kisses you give me
are always redemptions:
you kiss facing upward,
freeing something in me
that was still subject
to dark bottoms.
You save it, we see it
and see how it ascends
flying, impelled by you
into a paradise
where now it waits for us.
No, your flesh does not oppress
the earth it steps on
or my body you hold tight.
When you hug me I feel I held
a star against my chest,
throbbing,
not touching, very close,
that comes from another life.
The material world
is born when you leave.
And over my soul I feel
that enormous oppression
of shadows you left,
of lipless words
written on papers.
Now returned to the law
of metal, rock,

flesh. Your corporal
form,
your soft rose weight
is what turns me into
a world of lightness.
But what I can't hold up,
what pins me down,
calling me to the earth
without you to defend me,
is the distance, is
the hollow left by your body.

Yes. Never you, never you:
memory of you is matter.

46

How often I have been
—a spy of silence—
waiting for a word,
a voice. (Already known.
I knew them, yes,
but you, unaware of them,
had to tell them to me.)
Since the sound never came
I told them to myself,
I pronounced them alone,
for I missed them.
I hunted in alphabets
sleeping in the water,
in unused dictionaries
naked and ownerless,
for those loose letters
that you might put together
and did not tell me.
One day at last you spoke
but so deeply in the soul,
so remote,
that your voice was a pure
shadow of a voice, and I
never, never heard.

For I was stupidly
saying to myself
all I wanted to,
what you told me,
and what I would not
let myself hear.

47

Impossible to call her.
I did not sleep. She
thought I was sleeping.
And I let her do it all:
to go bit by bit
removing light
over my eyes;
to control footsteps,
breathing, changed
by her wish to be a shadow
that would never be in the way
with bulk and noise.
And to leave slowly,
slowly, taking the soul along,
so going out the door
she might leave behind
someone who could rest.
So as not to wake me,
me who was not sleeping.
And I could not call her.
To feel she wanted me,
wanting me then was
for her to go with others,
to talk loud, laugh,
but in the distance, safe
from my hearing her.
Finally free, cheerful,
picking butterflies
of foam, green ghosts
of olive trees, filled
with the pleasure of knowing me

in those arms of my dream
she gave me to—
never jealous
of her absence—
and I could not sleep.
Impossible to call her.
Her great work of love
was to leave me alone.

48

Night is the great doubt
of the world and of your love.
I need day
each day to tell me
it is day, that it is,
is light: and you are there.
The gigantic sinking
of marble and reeds,
the great blotting out
of wing and flower:
night, a threatening
abolition
of color and of you,
makes me tremble. Nothing there?
Did you once love me?
And while you are silent
and it is night, I don't know
if light and love exist.
I need the uncustomary
miracle: another day
and your voice confirming
the usual marvel.
And though you are silent,
in the enormous distance,
dawn at least,
dawn, yes. The light
it may give me today
will be the great yes of the world
to the love I have for you.

49

You can not love me:
you are loftily high!
And to console me
you send shadows, copies,
pictures, simulacra,
all so alike
as if they were you.
I live between images
of you, without you.
They like me,
go with me. We go
through cloisters of water,
through floating icebergs,
through the pampa or to deep
and diminutive movies.
Always talking about you.
They tell me:
"We're not exactly her but
if you could see how much alike!"
What long arms, hard
lips, your specters
have: yes, like you.
To act as if you cared,
they hug me and kiss me.
Their tender voices say
that you hug and kiss
like this. I live
on shadows, among shadows
of warm beautiful flesh,
with your eyes, your body,
kisses, yes, with all

of you except you.
With false creatures
mediating divinely
so that the great kiss
we cannot give each other
they give me, I give them.

50

The other one shows through you.
She looks like you:
her steps, the same frown,
same high heels
all stained with stars.
When the two of you go
down the street
how tricky it is to know
who you are, who is not you!
So much alike that it's
impossible to go on living
like that, so alike.
Since you are the fragile one,
scarcely existing, tender,
you must be the dead one.
You will let her kill you
so she may go on living,
lying, a fake you
but so alike
that no one but me
will remember what you were.
And one day
—it will come, yes, it will come—
when you look me in the eyes
you will see
that I think of her and love her:
you will see you are not you.

51

No, I can't believe
you are for me,
if you come near, if you come
and tell me: "I want you."
Can you love? You? Beauty
like a star or April
living above
the immense fate of loving,
in that immense altitude
where no one replies?
Will the sun or night
or a wave smile at me?
Does the world spin for me,
playing its seasons,
oranges, dry leaves?
They don't smile, spin
for me or for others.
Self-contained and cloistered
beauties want nothing
in their inexorable height.
They go out
casually, put on make up,
fly off, leaving behind
eager troupes
of longing and words.
They let themselves be loved, yes,
but never respond
with desire.
They flower, their leaves drop,
waves, grass, mornings:
pasture, for lambs,

children's games
and absolute silences.
But love for no one.
Only we, yes, we
loving. We the lovers.

52

Mirror, get her away from me.
Change her size.
Make her—who fills the world—
make her minute, minimal.
Let her fit in monosyllables,
in eyes,
so you can hold
that immeasurable
gazelle, captive now,
childlike in your frame.
Remove the ecstasy
of heat and volume
so that the last scales
won't feel her;
leave her cold, smooth,
buried in your quicksilver.
Deflect
her gaze; so she
won't see me, so she may think
she is alone.
That I may know finally
how she is when she is alone.
Give me from her
what she never gave me.
Though in this way
—what transparent truth!—
though in this way you take her from me.

53

Between your deepest truth
and me
you always place your kisses.
I sense it near,
desire it, don't reach it;
when I am closest to it
you block my way,
you offer your lips.
And I don't go any further.
You triumph. Kissing, I forget
your secret shut in a castle.
And you convert my longing
to go further toward you,
into desire
so you won't let me get away
and can kiss me.
Be careful.
You will get caught
like that. One day your kiss
will emerge
from so far, so deep,
that what you conceal
behind it
will spring fully into your lips.
And what you denied me
—thin and elusive soul—
will reach me, you will give it up
without wanting to,
where you meant to deny me.

54

The forehead is safer.
Lips give in, give up
their form to the other lip
that just kissed them.
We think
the world is squeezed in there,
the end and beginning:
they fool us without meaning to.
But the forehead is hard;
beneath the skin
is bone: stiff, eternal, an inflexible
answer, a monosyllable.
Worlds ripen
behind that fortress.
Nothing can be seen
or touched. Pink
or dark skin
lightly masks
the absolute defense
of ultimate being. You
surrender kisses and essential
sweetness in the world
in a round fruit,
here on lips. But
when I touch your forehead
with my forehead, I feel you
the most distant lover,
furthest away,
that will last secretly
when lips

and kisses pass. Salvation
—cold, hard in the earth—
of the great ardent contact
that burns this night.

55

Not to ask you, saves me.
If I did ask
before you said anything,
how clear it would all be,
all over with now!
It would be to change your arms,
your dawns—indecisive
where they are going—
to change the doubt
where you live, where I live
as in a great unlit world,
for a cold bright
coin: the truth.
You would go off then.
Where your body now is,
vacillating, trembling
about kissing me or not,
would be certainty: your lipless
absence. And where now
are anguish, torment,
skies black with possible
stars, with chance,
would be only she alone.
Now, always: my only lover.
I beside you without you.
I alone with the truth.

56

I am forming your shadow.
Now I have it without those
red and hard lips: they were burning.
I would have kissed them
even more.

Then I parry your quick,
long nervous arms.
They offered me the road
so I could grab hold.

I pull out color, mass.
I kill off your step. You were coming
right to me. What hurt me most
when I silenced it
is your voice. Rich, so warm,
more palpable than your body.
But it was set to betray us.

So
my love is free, loose,
with your bodiless shadow.
And I can live in you
with no fear
of what I most desire,
of your kiss, your arms.
To be always brooding
on your lips, your voice,
body
that I stripped from you
so now without them
I can love you.

And how I wanted them!
And to hold, not stopping, painlessly
(while your flesh goes
on its own road, detached,
my great love behind)
your only possible body:
your sweet imagined body.

57

Tell me, why that thirst
to make you possible
when you know you are
one who will never be?
You at my side, in your flesh,
in your body, are only
the great crazy wish
to be here at my side
in your body, in your flesh.
In everything you do
true, visible,
nothing is flaming
or accomplished. No.
What you do is just
what you want to do,
doing it.
The words, hands
you let me have, I kiss
through your own unrealizable will
of giving as you give.
And the closer you come
to me and deeper you press
against the indestructible and black
no, the vaster
in your thirst to abolish them,
to make them not be
are the hollow distances

you like to ignore
when you hug me. I feel
that your life in me
is pure label, signals
in kisses, presences
of your impossible
wish to live
with me, mine, always.

58

I looked for you through doubt:
never found you.

I went to meet you
through pain.
You didn't come that way.

I got into the very bottom
to see if, finally, you were there.
Through anguish
ripping, wounding me.
You never came out of the incision.

And no one gave me a hint
—a garden or your lips
with trees, with kisses—
no one told me
—that's why I lost you—
that you were moving through the last
terraces of laughter,
of pleasure, of what is sure.
That you were really
on the peaks of a kiss,
unalarmed, with no future.
On the steep vertex
of tall joy,
multiplying ecstasy
by ecstasy, by laughter,
by pleasure.
That you were jotting down
fabulous airy ciphers on the air
of your joy.

59

One gets to you only
through you. I wait for you.

Yes I know where I am,
my city, street, the name
they all call me.
But I don't know where I was
with you.
You took me there.

How
was I to find out the road
when I was looking at nothing
but you,
when the road was your walk,
and the end
was when you stopped?
What more could I have than
what you offered gazing at me?
But now
what exile, what absence
it is to be where one is!
I wait. Trains go by,
chances, looks.
They would take me where
I've never been. But I
don't want new skies.
I want to be where I was.
With you, to be back.
What an immense newness
to go back again,

to repeat the never same
infinite wonder!
And while you don't come
I'll stay on the shore
of flights, dreams,
still, behind ship foam.
For I know that no wings,
wheels, sails take me where
I was.
All wander off.
For I know that where I was
one gets to you only
through you.

60

You can't see them.
I can.
Bright, round, lukewarm.
Slowly
they go off to their destiny;
slowly to delay
leaving your flesh.
They go nowhere; they are
just that, their flow.
And a long trail
immediately rubbed out.
Stars?

You
can't kiss them.
I kiss them for you.
They taste. They've got the taste
of the world's juices.
What a black thick taste
of earth, sun, sea!
They stick a second
in a kiss—drawn
between your chilly flesh
and my lips; finally
I rip them out. And I don't know
if they were for me.
For I know nothing.
Are they stars, signals,
penalties or daybreaks?
I found out nothing
in looking or kissing.

What they want stays
there behind, a mystery.
And their name too.
(If I called them tears
no one would catch on.)

61

If you knew that this
sob confined to
your arms, that
tear you dry
kissing it,
come from you, are you,
pain from you turned into water,
my sobs!

Then
you would not ask
the past, skies,
forehead, letters,
what's wrong, why I suffer.
And quiet,
with that quietness
of light and knowledge,
you would kiss me more,
desolately,
with a desolation
that has no other being or pain
beside it—one alone
with pain—
trying to help some other
chimera's
sorrow.

62

When you chose me
—love chose—
I came out of the great anonymity,
from all and from nothing.
Till then
I was never taller than
the sierras of the world.
I never sank deeper
than the maximum
depths marked out
on maritime charts.
And my gladness was
sad, like small watches
with no wrist to fasten to,
that stop, unwound.
But when you said "you"
to me, yes, to me singled out—
I was higher than stars,
deeper than coral.
And my joy
began to spin, caught
in your being, in your pulse.
You gave me possession of myself
when you gave your self to me.
I lived. I live. How long?
I know you will back out.
When you go
I will go back to a deaf
world that does not distinguish
gram or drop
in weight or water.

I'll be one more—like the rest—
when you are lost.
I'll lose my name,
my age, my gestures, all
lost in me, from me.
Gone back to the immense bone heap
of those who have not died
and now have no death to die
in life.

63

I don't want you to go,
pain, last form
of loving. I feel myself
live when you hurt me
not in you, not here, but far off:
in land and the year
where you come from,
in her love
and all that was.
In that drowned
reality that denies
itself and claims
it never was,
that it was only my
pretext for living.
If you did not stick with me,
irrefutable sorrow,
I might agree.
But you stay.
Your truth assures me
that nothing was a lie.
Pain, while I feel you,
you will be
proof of another life
when you did not ache.
The great proof, far,
that she was, that she is,
that she loved me, yes
that I still love her.

64

What gigantic weight,
celestial bodies
—wonder, miracle—
are supported by
winds, absences,
paper, nothing!
Rock rests on rock,
bodies lie in cradles,
in tombs; islands don't
fool us, fictions
of false paradise
floating over the water.
But you, you, memory
of a past that was gentle
flesh, live matter
and now is nothing
but infinite weight,
gravity, oppression,
tell me, who holds you up
if it is not the hoped-for
solitude of the night?
And you, hunger
for return,
unvarying,
precisely the same,
of fresh new actions
we call future,
who can hold you up?
Signs and semblances
traced on white, green, blue
scraps of paper

want to be your eternal
support, to be your floor,
your promised earth.
But then, later,
hands tear them up,
they vanish into time,
dust, leaving only vague
illusive traces,
memories in the soul.
Yes, souls, the ends!
The ultimate, always
select, weak,
eternal fulcrum
of the heaviest weights.
Souls like wings
upheld by
desperate movement,
by never stopping,
by flying, carriers
through the air, in the air,
of salvation.

65

Not in marble palaces,
not in months, no, nor in ciphers
never touching the floor:
we have lived together
in fragile delicate worlds.
Time was scarcely
counted in minutes;
a minute was a century,
a life, a love.
Roofs sheltered us,
they were less
roofs than clouds,
less clouds than skies,
they were air, nothing.
Crossing oceans
made of twenty tears,
ten yours and ten mine,
we came to gold
necklace beads,
clean islands free
of flowers and beasts;
a tiny glass
harbor of love
enough
for the biggest love,
and it asked
no help from ships or time.
Enormous galleries
opening
into grains of sand,
where we discovered mines

of fire and surprise.
And all
hanging from a thread
that was holding up—who?
That's why our life
does not seem lived:
it slipped away,
no wake or steps
behind. If you want
to recall it, don't gaze
where one always looks
for traces and memory.
Don't look at the soul,
at shadow, at lips.
Look carefully into
the empty palm of your hand.

66

Yes, we will find it.
Our kiss. Maybe
in a bed of clouds,
of glass or burning coals.
Maybe
in the next minute
or tomorrow or in the coming
century or on the very edge
of what is never.
Live, dead? Do you know?
With your flesh and mine,
my name and yours?
Or must it now be with
other lips, other names
and centuries after
what longs to be
today, here, from now on?
We don't know that.
We know it will be.
In something, yes, in someone
will come
a love we invented
without land or date
where it can be now.
A huge love in the air.
And maybe from behind
the curtain of years,
will come
a kiss under never seen skies,
unknown to those
who think they are kissing,

rising into luminosity,
to achieve at last
that impatient kiss
I see you waiting for,
throbbing in your lips.
Today
our kiss, its bed,
lies only in faith.

67

Who? Who can people the world
for me on this August night?
No. Neither body nor soul.
Gas lights against the moon.
Hug me? Who?
Pursue her? Whom? Rapid
coincidences of star
and gas take the place.
Shadows and me. And air
blandly swaying
the shadow's hair
with a sound of soul.
I will go to her bed
—quiet air, quiet water—
to try to make them want me
through silence
and kiss. Tricked
until the day comes
and the big empty bed
where they were sleeping
with no sign of flesh
in the clean void
of air, when
(with no sign from the soul)
they will again confirm
my solitude, saying
that it was all quick
meetings, here under
far lights,
an unresponding gamble.
No. No flesh, no souls.

68

What subtile light bodies
there are,
colorless, inconcrete like shadows,
that can't be kissed
except by putting your lips
in the air, against something
passing by and that resembles them!

And what brown shadows,
so hard
that their cold dark marble
will never fall
passionately in our arms!

And what going and coming,
with love flying about,
from bodies to shadows,
from impossibility to lips,
ceaselessly, never knowing
if it is soul, flesh, or shadow
of a body that we kiss,
if anything at all! Terrified
of caressing nothing!

69

If shadows were not
shadows? If shadows were
—I grab them, kiss them,
they burn me shaking
in their arms—
slim fine bodies,
all frightened of flesh?

And if there were
other light in the world
to draw out of them
bodies of shade, other
more complete ghosts, empty
of color, form, free
of the suspicion of matter;
and unseen,
that one could look for
blind through the heavens,
now despising others,
and not hear voices
from those masked bodies
of shadows on the earth?

70

Do you hear how they beg for realities,
those dishevelled terrible
shadows that we both make up
in this great bed of distances?
Tired now of infinity, of loose
time, of anonymity, and wounds
from an intense nostalgia for matter,
they ask for limits, days, names.
They can't
live this way any longer: they are at the edge
of the death of shadows, that is nothingness.
Come near, come with me.
Stretch out your hands, offer them your body.
We two will look for a color
for them, a date, a chest, a sun.
Let them relax in you, you be their flesh.
Their enormous roaming hunger will calm
while we clutch them
greedily between our bodies
where they will find pasture and repose.
They will sleep at last in our dream,
in our embrace. And so, then,
when we go apart, when we nourish ourselves only
with shadows, caught in distances,
they will have memories, a past
of flesh and bone:
the time when they lived in us.
And their starving dream
of shadows will be the return again
to a mortal and rose body
where love invents its infinity.